Essentialism

And the Art of Not Giving a Fuck

By Stephen Parato

Essentialism

The key to success, the key to peace of mind, the key to making your dreams come true ultimately boils down to one thing: *focusing on the essential*.

What is "essential" can be different for everyone. For some people, that may be their family, for others it may be music, for some people it may be travel. It all depends on what you want to prioritize in your life.

What are your priorities? What do you want to focus on? What is your purpose? What direction do you want to travel in? In order to make the most out of life, we must ask ourselves those questions and prioritize accordingly.

If you don't have priorities or purpose, then you will fritter away your days in a muck of endless distractions, yet be left feeling empty inside. Without focus, the world around you has more than enough distractions to keep you preoccupied, passive, stagnant and depressingly mediocre.

Let go of the unessential and cut out distractions. If you want to write a book, watching tv for 2 hours a day won't help. If you want to get in shape, prioritize your workouts and healthy meals. If you want to be a better parent, spend more quality time with your kids by any means necessary. Find out what is essential to you and let go of the unessential.

This applies to everything in life, from business to relationships and everything in between. A company will be successful if it focuses on its core mission. A relationship will be harmonious if both people place love first.

Make *Essentialism* an "essential" part of your life, and help bring your dreams to fruition.

This is Essentialism And the Art of Not Giving a Fuck.

The Balance

This book is actually about doing less, letting go of the unessential. In fact, we all have a lot to learn from a bit of "nothingness."

Nothingness is the infinity from which everything arises. Space is the canvas which births form. Silence provides context for music. Rest supports activity. You get the idea. And honestly, we can't "do nothing" for the rest of our lives. Even existing as a human is SOMETHING. Yet we can acquaint with this space and receive the benefits of simplicity.

Most of us can greatly benefit by clearing our minds, relaxing and having some space to think, feel and just... BE. You see, today's world is on the extreme of mindless activity. It doesn't take a genius to see that this isn't an optimal way of approaching life.

Here's how this fits in with the phrase "not giving a fuck." Giving a fuck is being consumed by unconscious mental chatter, anxiety, distraction - and above all, fear. Not giving a fuck is letting go of everything that doesn't serve you, transcending fears and focusing on what is essential to you.

Another key point is that not giving a fuck means focusing on the essential without attachment. Meaning you still have things that are important to you, yet you're not attached to the outcome.

Not giving a fuck (applied to Essentialism) = Focusing on the essential, without fear or attachment.

If you're reading this, chances are you're more towards the side of mindless activity and could use a healthy dose of nothingness. And by nothingness, I don't mean spending the rest of your life watching tv. That's something! And far from the best something, which we'll get into. I'm talking about taking a deep inhale and literally becoming that peaceful space before the exhale. I'm talking about letting go of all of the unnecessary burdens, fears, doubts, worries, anger, jealousy, insecurities, delusions, shoulds and shouldn'ts, guilt, limiting beliefs, false constructs, biases, comparisons, neuroses, personality masks, jaw-clenching frustration, foot stomping impatience and "Why didn't they text me back?"-s you're hanging onto.

For a more enjoyable, peaceful and harmonious life as individuals – and consequently as a species – we must learn balance. Right now, we're tipping the scales towards the side of mindless activity. It's time to release some of the burdensome weight from that side…

The Attachment Trap

"The root of all suffering is attachment." – Buddha

Attachment is based in fear. Think about it. You're attached to your lover because you're afraid they'll leave. You're attached to your job because you're afraid of not making money. You're attached to your identity because your ego is afraid to just BE. You're attached to an idea because you're afraid of being wrong. You're attached to everything you have because you're afraid of what's outside of your comfort zone. Can you see the trend?

So in many ways, attachment is "giving too many fucks."

Now you might be saying, *"Hold on! Are you telling me I shouldn't care about anything?"*

Nope. All I'm saying is to release attachments.

You can still love someone without being attached to them. In fact, true love has nothing to do with attachment. It is unconditional and freeing. You can still do incredible work without being attached to it. I'm doing that while writing this book. You can still make a positive impact on the world without being attached to the results. In fact, nonattachment increases the quality of everything you do.

The art of giving a fuck is all about transcending fear and attachment. When you clear all of the bullshit you've accumulated throughout life, what are you left with? Peace, love, happiness and bliss.

And that's what we're all chasing – some combination of those feelings – right?

Back to the Basics

We need some basic things for survival: air, water, food, shelter, clothing and love. Even clothing is only really necessary when it's cold.

Besides our basic survival NEEDS, everything else is a conditioned WANT. I'm not saying that everyone should throw away everything and have no desires. I'm saying to simply be aware that, except for your survival needs, everything else is a want. And many people have confused their wants for needs, which creates a mind filled with expectations that are often never met.

Life can become unnecessarily burdensome when we confuse our wants with our needs. When you think you need a cup of coffee in the morning, but you don't get it, what happens? Do you get frustrated? Do you resist what's happening and wish you had the coffee? It's not a need. If it doesn't happen, it doesn't happen. Let go. Life goes on.

Once your survival needs are met, everything else is a bonus. Learn to consciously enjoy those bonuses without attaching to them.

Wisdom From Michelangelo

"Beauty is the purgation of superfluities." – Michelangelo

This quote by Michelangelo epitomizes the idea of Essentialism. What the Renaissance man meant by that poetic phrase was this: beauty is the removal of the unnecessary.

All aspects of beauty, all aspects of a beautiful life, simply emerge when we let go of the useless excess. When fear is let go of, we're left with happiness. When we transcend limiting beliefs, success greets us. When we remove our blocks, creative inspiration flows.

Michelangelo also said the following regarding his artwork...*"I saw the angel in the marble and carved until I set him free."* This further shows how, in his genius, he used reductionism to create great art.

This "Michelangelo mindstate" applies to everything in life. Even if not literally with certain things, it applies metaphorically.

So let's extrapolate a bit. How do you think Michelangelo would have approached modern life? If I were to guess, it would be very similar to this concept of Essentialism.

Removing the Unnecessary

Most of us think that more is synonymous with better. We think we need to keep adding things in order to be happy or to have a good life.

Here's the truth, it's actually the removal of the unnecessary that creates happiness and allows us to live the life of our dreams.

Let's take a simple example. Most people would like to travel the world, but they have all of the same excuses... *"I can't quit my job. I have all of these bills. I have a house with a mortgage. I have a car. I have so much that's keeping me rooted here."* Can you see? These are all things weighing someone down, preventing them from traveling the world. The actual "doing it" is the easy part. Anyone reading this can buy a plane ticket, even if they have to put it on a credit card. The point is that the "stuff" we've accumulated in every aspect of life is what prevents us from living the life we truly want.

Another layer of barriers are the fears we have. Fear comes in many forms. And once fear is removed, things just start flowing towards us. Take away the underlying fears of talking to that pretty guy or girl, and the action just happens. Take away the fear of failing, and you can't help but take more chances. Take away the fear of the unknown, and your feet just start to move toward adventure. Take away your excuses not to do something, and it gets done almost effortlessly.

Of course, action is required for most things. But action becomes unforced and almost effortless once we let go of all of the unnecessary.

Before we can grow into our full potential, we must first address the forces that are holding us back...

The Information Overload Age

We live in the information age.

It's a beautiful thing. It really is. We have access to more information right now than kings had in their entire lifetimes. That's extremely powerful.

Over the last few years, we've been able to share more information than ever before. No one can be ignorant now, for better or worse (unless they consciously choose to be ignorant). The playing field has been leveled and there is no longer a monopoly on information. It's all becoming open-sourced.

Here's why information is so important. Things need to be known before they can be changed. Information is potential power. And applied information is power.

Yet every tool is a double-edged sword. With this almost limitless access to information comes its shadow side. We're learning how to integrate this new way of living and find our balance with it. This is why many people are suffering from information overwhelm. It's constant and all-pervasive. This is adding to stresses, anxieties, worry, addictive patterns, short attention spans, lack of focus, indecisiveness...etc.

If we don't know how to consciously navigate our way through the ocean of information, we'll surely drown. As a collective, we're learning how to swim by jumping into the water head first.

The key to mastering the information age is to simplify and consciously seek out information. Otherwise, you will drown. A lack of purpose, a lack of mindfulness, will only result in overwhelm.

Be the King/Queen of the domain of your own mind. Keep information in formation.

The "News" (Aka Overloading the Mind With Fear)

The so-called "news" is a topic we simply can't afford to tiptoe around. Not only that, it's one of the "low hanging fruits" to eliminate that will instantly enhance your quality of life.

Let me start by saying that most successful people, in any aspect of life, don't fritter away their days by watching the news. Why? Because they're focused on their mission! If you have a purpose, if you're working towards something that makes the world a better place, what good does it do you to watch the news? If anything, it's going to hinder your ability to create.

Most people can agree that the news is a massive perpetuator of fear. Right?

This is the main point here: Watching the news and marinating in fear will not allow you to be the best version of yourself or help others to the best of your ability.

Think about this, have you ever felt good after watching the news? I haven't. Watching the news is like drowning in a flood of all the woes of the world. I'm not saying to ignore things or to not have compassion. I'm saying to focus on your mission and what you can do to make the world a better place. Yes, bad things are happening everywhere, but what can you do about it? You can focus on your mission and uplift those you encounter every day. That's much more productive to focus on.

Many will counter this by saying, *"But I need to stay informed."* Sure, it's important to be aware. But much of the news is heavily biased, not very truthful and not at all actionable. We want to maximize our ability to positively impact the world, based on a grounded foundation. The news does not provide us with this.

The news provides little to no context for what is reported. It just gives us a horrific event, without explaining what led to it, which elicits a predictable response of fear, sadness or outrage within people. For the most part, it's third grade reading level fear mongering. Yes, good journalism does exist, but the mainstream media, especially in the US, is very far from it.

The "News" (Part 2)

Everyone can agree that the news cherry picks all of the "bad stuff" in the world.

It creates more hype. And people are more easily controlled when they're in fear. A state of fear shuts down the brain's higher functions and activates the amygdala, which is the fight or flight part of the brain. This puts people in a state where they irrationally and illogically react to things. Can you see that this happens with people when they watch the news? Have you noticed this with yourself? I definitely have.

Without going down conspiracy theory rabbit holes, just know that 90% of the US media is controlled by 6 companies and they do not have your best interest in mind. They want profits and control, and your well-being does not fit into that agenda.

If you start your day by watching the news, are you going to be able to be the best version of yourself to the people you encounter? Nope. You're going to be fearful, paranoid, worried, anxious, irritated, angry...etc.

Instead of watching the news, start your day by meditating or stretching (we'll get into morning routines later). Then go into your day focusing on your purpose and helping as many people as possible. Don't underestimate this. Engaging in a peaceful, healthy morning routine has a profound impact on quality of life.

If you don't have a purpose, then what are you doing with your life? Start asking those questions. If you're floundering, there will always be an authority figure that will gladly step up and tell you what to do. I don't know about you, but I value the freedom to make my own choices.

So here's the solution. Get in touch with why you're on this planet. Discover (or create) your purpose and work towards that. If something is big enough news, you'll hear about it from your friends, family or people around you.

You're not going to change the world by watching the news and worrying. However, you will play a part in changing the world by working on yourself, finding peace within, carrying out your mission and being kind to people on a daily basis.

Gandhi said, *"Be the change you wish to see in the world."* He didn't say, *"Watch the news every day and complain about everything you can't change."*

If you want to simplify your life; if you want to focus on what is truly essential; if you want peace of mind; if you want to maximize your positive impact on the world... Stop watching the news.

Just by letting go of something as simple (yet insidious) as the news, you will free up so much time, creativity and peace of mind that you didn't even realize were being stifled by fear and anxiety.

Circle of Concern vs Circle of Control

Your circle of concern consists of everything within your awareness. Anything that you're aware of is in your circle of concern. This can be news events, your friend posting pictures of their travels on social media, what the president of the United States said yesterday, what happened in the last episode of your favorite tv show, that person who yelled at you in traffic…etc. All of that stuff.

Your circle of control is what you can actually control. You have control over the thoughts you choose, the actions you choose and the reactions you choose. That's pretty much it.

Most people focus on their circle of concern and neglect their circle of control. This is insanity! And because so many people do this, it makes things worse on the collective level. Because so many people live in fear and believe that their daily actions are meaningless.

It's all about where your focus is. If you focus on your circle of concern, you become passive. And because most things on the news or tv are not empowering, it's most likely going to be passive and negative. This is the state most people are in. If you don't focus on your circle of control, you're going to be a victim. It's that simple.

Are you going to be a passive victim or are you going to be responsible and empowered? That's the question you have to ask yourself. You might not be able to change what the President said at a press conference, but you can change your own thoughts, actions and reactions.

Again, this is where a sense of purpose comes in. What do you want to do? What impact do you want to have? What ripple do you want to send across the Universe?

You can optimize your health. You can write a book that inspires people. You can smile at a stranger on the street. You can hold the door open for someone. You can give a genuine compliment. You can support local businesses. You can choose inner peace. You can start a business that creates positive change in the world. You can create art that brings people joy. All of these are possible for anyone, but they require you to focus on your circle of control.

Wisdom from Lao Tzu

"Sometimes gain comes from losing, and sometimes loss comes from gaining."

"To attain knowledge, add things every day. To attain wisdom, remove things every day."

"By letting go it all gets done."

"Stop leaving and you will arrive. Stop searching and you will see. Stop running away and you will be found."

"We shape clay into a pot, but it is the emptiness inside that holds whatever we want."

"Who acts in stillness finds stillness in his life."

"Doing nothing is better than being busy doing nothing."

"Nature does not hurry, yet everything is accomplished."

"Simplicity, patience, compassion.
These three are your greatest treasures.
Simple in actions and thoughts, you return to the source of being.
Patient with both friends and enemies,
you accord with the way things are.
Compassionate toward yourself,
you reconcile all beings in the world."

The Myth of Television and Relaxation

We discussed the news. Now it's time to get into television in general. On average, American adults watch five hours of tv every day. That is absolutely insane!

If you think about it, everything you watch on tv is in your circle of concern, not in your circle of control. This is why so many people feel disempowered and like they're on the periphery of life, while giving all of their power to politicians, celebrities and tv personalities. Imagine dedicating five hours per day towards a passion or a purpose? Hello mastery!

Many people watch tv because they want to "relax" after a day of work. And that's completely understandable. But here's the thing: Television is not actually relaxing.

EEG studies show that the higher-functioning levels of the brain, like the neocortex we use for analysis and reasoning, go offline when we zone out in front of the screen. Meanwhile the visual cortex is highly stimulated. This leaves the brain in a weird limbo where neurons are still firing but the mind is not actually engaged. It's taking in a lot of information but is not processing it, so the brain isn't relaxed, but it's not being exercised either.

Television creates a situation where parts of your brain are highly stimulated, your logical facilities are offline, and you're passively sitting down watching. So if you're watching anything remotely action-packed or stimulating (which is most of what's on tv), your body is going to be in fight or flight mode and producing stress hormones. And because you're just sitting there, the stress is festering in your body. This is far different than the stress of exercising, for example, because with exercise your body is actually moving.

Here's a quote from Scientific American:
"Survey participants commonly reflect that television has somehow absorbed or sucked out their energy, leaving them depleted. They say they have more difficulty concentrating after viewing than before. In contrast, they rarely indicate such difficulty after reading. After playing sports or engaging in hobbies, people report improvements in mood. After watching TV, people's moods are about the same or worse than before."

Television and Hypnosis

What do you get when higher brain function (logic and reasoning) is shut down, yet the visual cortex is highly stimulated? You get the perfect recipe for subconscious programming and hypnosis.

When watching television, your brain waves are brought to a low alpha range, which is associated with meditation and deep relaxation. In this low alpha range, your conscious mind is essentially shut off and all input goes straight to your subconscious mind. This can be dangerous if you're absorbing any less than optimal input. Our deepest beliefs and patterned behaviors come from our subconscious mind. So we must be diligent as to what goes into our subconsciousness (if you care about your well-being).

The low alpha waves entrain your brain for the greatest suggestibility. And it gets worse too. Your mind gets confused and derailed by the condensed and unrealistic story lines of many shows. The imagery creates an influx of stress hormones – like a constant release of adrenaline – but with no outlet because you're just sitting there. We consciously try to tell ourselves that it's just a show but our subconscious mind does not differentiate between perceived and experienced reality. Everything we watch and experience gets soaked up by the subconscious mind and influences our beliefs and behavior.

Think about how suggestible people are under hypnosis. If you've seen a good hypnotist, it's pretty crazy right? Well, our brains are operating on the same frequency while watching television. And because of this, we're highly suggestible to whatever is shown on the tv.

There is so much on television that is not in your best interest to subject yourself to: From the manufactured desires of consumerism created by commercials, to picking up all of the stress of a tv drama, to the fear-based programming of the news.

The bottom line is to reduce or eliminate tv watching. If you want to be as happy, healthy, helpful, successful and impactful as possible, you need to be mindful of what you're absorbing subconsciously. Focus on what is essential to you.

What are you programming yourself with? Drama, fear, crime, commercials and consumerism? Or are you purposefully feeding your subconscious mind with love, compassion, empowerment, courage, harmony and peace? You reap what you sew into your subconscious mind. The choice is up to you.

Note: Television programs are programming mechanisms. News anchors are people who anchor hypnotic suggestions. Anchoring is a term in hypnosis for creating a stimulus (behavior) that is associated with a particular state of mind or mood. It's all in the language!

Social Media and Internet Rabbit Holes

As of 2017, the average amount of time people spend on social media is two hours every day. And people spend a lot more time that that on the internet in general.

That's a lot of time.

And not only do we get *information overload* because of this, we also get *opinion overload*. Meaning that we're subjected to so many other people's opinions that it becomes difficult to focus on what is important to us.

I'm definitely not advocating giving up social media and the internet entirely. Both have tremendous advantages and create possibilities that were unimaginable 30 years ago.

However, I do believe that two things will allow you to leverage the benefits and avoid the pitfalls:
- Reduce the Amount of Time
- Mindful Use

Reducing the amount of time you spend on the internet and social media will undoubtedly benefit most people. To do this, I recommend ***intermittent technological fasting***. What I mean by this is taking a break from technology on a regular basis. Here are a few ideas:
- Don't use technology after a certain time at night – Not using technology after 9PM, for example, will help you relax and sleep.
- Don't use technology during the first hour of waking – Ease into your morning, engage in a morning routine and cultivate peace before diving into the world of chaos and distraction.
- Take a day off from technology - Maybe even to this once a week. I like to do "Screen Free Sundays" every few weeks.

Note: By technology, I basically mean smartphones, computers and tv.

And then we have mindful use of technology. Limiting the time you spend on your phone or computer will automatically create more mindfulness for you. If you take technology breaks regularly, you'll break the default patterning. This means you'll be less likely to mindlessly look at your phone or scroll through Facebook for 20 minutes for no reason.

Do it On Purpose

Awareness is crucial. It's so easy to get lost if you're not mindful. It's so easy to get distracted.

Be mindful of your social media and internet use.

Here's a powerful strategy to cultivate mindfulness... Every time you "check in" ask yourself, *"What is my purpose here?"*

Is it to research something? Is it to share something? Is it to see what your friends are up to? Or is it to distract yourself because you're bored? Build the habit of asking yourself, *"What is my purpose here?"*

Simply asking yourself why you're doing it will create awareness around your behavior. I don't know about you, but I don't feel good after I mindlessly scroll through social media feeds, only to find that I wasted the last hour distracting myself with nonsense.

Another strategy is to implement a **No Scroll Rule**. Every time you go on the internet or social media, make sure you have a purpose. Don't just scroll through. When you scroll through a newsfeed or a website, what you're doing is just looking for something to distract you.

Use technology with purpose. Technology is incredibly powerful when used with purpose, but incredibly detrimental when used mindlessly and for distraction. The choice is up to you.

State your purpose. Are you going on Facebook to post a picture? Post the picture and then leave. Are you going on the internet to look up a coffee shop nearby? Find it and be done.

Whatever you do, it's absolutely crucial to be aware and mindful. Awareness is the first step of any change, and it's transformative in and of itself.

The key is mindfulness. Unlock your peace of mind. Open the door to your full potential.

Distraction and Focus

All of the distractions we've discussed so far – tv, news, social media, smartphones – hinder your ability to focus.

The brain adapts. So if we feed it distraction from all angles, we gradually lose the ability to focus.

The average human attention span has fallen from 12 seconds in 2000, or around the time the mobile revolution began, to eight seconds. Goldfish, meanwhile, are believed to have an attention span of nine seconds.

How crazy is that?

Because of this, most people have a hard time doing anything that necessitates prolonged focus. How are you going to learn a new skill? How are you going to create anything? How are you going to master anything without focus?

You can feel the difference too. It doesn't feel good to realize that you're just scrolled through Facebook for an hour. But it does feel good to write, read a book, build something or do anything that requires focus for the same period of time.

Being constantly distracted and scatterbrained results in anxiety, depression, restlessness and lack of peace in the present moment. We all know this, we all feel it, yet few of us do anything to change it.

Do one thing at a time. It's a muscle, like everything else. Start small but keep at it.

Learn to transcend the onslaught of triviality and focus on the essential.

The Low Information Diet

The low information diet is the solution to everything we just discussed.

Here's what the low information diet is in a nutshell: *Reducing your consumption of information - both the amount of sources and the sheer volume of information – and focusing on the essential.* This means that you have to be diligent and very intentional with all of the information you consume.

It's about minimal and mindful consumption of information, as opposed to the mindless overconsumption of information that pervades our culture. Make sure that the information you choose to consume has a purpose, and you're not just doing it mindlessly or to distract yourself. That purpose could be as intellectual as learning more about physics, or as simple as finding something humorous. The key here is being purposeful and mindful.

A low information diet requires you to reduce (or preferably eliminate) news and television. And only use the following if it has a purpose: social media, online articles, magazines...etc.

Just doing this will free up tremendous amounts of time and energy. It will provide you with space. And this space is where the magic happens. Do not fill the void with more distractions; nourish the space with meditation, walking outside or anything that allows you to just BE!

We'll get into more ways to leverage this space later, but just know that this space is where insights, ideas, creativity and everything you create in the world comes from. Without this space, you will be unable to create anything or blossom into your full potential. If you can't do these things, you're stifling your ability to positively impact yourself and the world at large.

Wisdom from Bruce Lee

"It's not the daily increase but daily decrease. Hack away at the unessential."

"The less effort, the faster and more powerful you will be."

"Empty your cup so that it may be filled; become devoid to gain totality."

"I fear not the man who has practiced 10,000 kicks once, but I fear the man who has practiced one kick 10,000 times."

"If you love life, don't waste time, for time is what life is made up of."

"Adapt what is useful, reject what is useless, and add what is specifically your own."

"The more we value things, the less we value ourselves."

"Be self-aware, rather than a repetitious robot."

"To spend time is to pass it in a specified manner. To waste time is to expend it thoughtlessly or carelessly. We all have time to either spend or waste and it is our decision what to do with it. But once passed, it is gone forever."

The Busy Syndrome

So many of us wear "busyness" like a badge of honor. It has become a semi-depressing bragging right.

If you find yourself constantly saying "I'm busy," take a step back for a moment and ask this question... "Am I focusing on what really matters?"

In today's frantically-paced society, we're becoming increasingly time-stressed. The insidious state of time-poverty has people in a vice grip, to the point that families spend only eight hours per week together on average. And most of that time is spent in front of the television. That's a disturbing symptom of something being fundamentally wrong.

Look around you. Most people are in a perpetual state of running around like a chicken with their head cut off. Tense faces, taut bodies and hurried movement are the dominant characteristics. Rest? Leisure? Meditation? A walk in the woods? Meaningful conversations with loved ones? In the words of YouTube sensation Sweet Brown, "Ain't nobody got time for that." So they think...

We've become the life equivalent of those awkward, neurotic gym-goers; thrusting ourselves in a spastic rehearsal of jerking rapidity, with no concern for technique, let alone the perspective to evaluate if we're even performing the correct exercise.

Doing more and more, faster and faster, has become the unspoken mantra in today's society. And it couldn't be more misguided.

Let's take sprinting (which, by the way, is completely based on producing maximum speed) as an example. Do sprinters sprint 24/7? Of course not. They have carefully calculated training programs, with rest being equally as important as the actual training. Sprinters also spend the overwhelming majority of their time resting. Even their training sessions, which include short bursts of high intensity sprinting, ae mixed with much longer periods of rest. If an athlete attempted to sprint all day, they would quickly tire, and within minutes be relegated to crawling around the track.

But this is how many people try to move through life. In a desperate attempt to keep pushing, they end up at an incessant, exhausting crawl with no time to rest (so they think), no energy left to move at full speed and no clarity to even question why they're doing it in the first place.

Here's a little secret. If you learn to be still, build awareness and periodically take strategic, powerful action, you'll actually accomplish far more, while maintaining your inner peace. How does that sound?

It's all really simple. Get clear about what you want, prioritize it, let go of the unessential and give yourself some space. In doing so, you will get more done with less stress.

Anxiety Society

Due to a wide variety of factors, we have an "anxiety society."

Most people are anxious far more often than they are at peace. This is not a fun way to live; not at all. But it doesn't have to be this way.

I've suffered from soul-crushing anxiety myself. I remember when a constant state of anxiety was my normal. I would play out future scenarios and miss out on the present moment. I would carefully avoid uncomfortable situations. And I would drink alcohol until I was numb to the anxiety.

Yet when there's life, there's hope. I slowly dug myself out of this hole using many of the principles I lay out in this book.

There are 3 levels as to why anxiety is such a problem these days:
1. Mental-Emotional
2. Physical
3. Spiritual

On the mental-emotional level, we're constantly stressed and under pressure. Oftentimes, our self-worth and identity is attached to how much we do. Combine this with the insidious busy syndrome and we have masses of people looking for salvation somewhere in the future, and completely neglecting the present moment. The future is useful for planning, but it ultimately exists in the mind. If you live too much in the future, you'll suffer from anxiety. Think of anxiety as the chasm between your mind (living in the future) and your body (in the present moment). Close this chasm and watch anxiety fade away.

Then we have the physical level. One of the more surprising links is the relationship between the gut microbiome and brain function. Recent studies have shown that there's a definite link between gut health and anxiety. Mental health and mood are negatively affected by a lack of "good" gut bacteria. So optimizing your gut flora will help reduce or even eliminate anxiety. Holistic health practitioners have long said that gut health is intimately tied to mental health. Before the science backed it up, it was dismissed as quackery. But now the science strongly supports those assertions.

Dr. Joseph Mercola explains the connection well:

"To put this into more concrete terms, you've probably experienced the visceral sensation of butterflies in your stomach when you're nervous, or had an upset stomach when you were very angry or stressed. The flip side is also true, in that problems in your gut can directly impact your mental health, leading to issues like anxiety, depression, and autism."

And here's what Scientific American has to say:

"The gut-brain axis seems to be bidirectional—the brain acts on gastrointestinal and immune functions that help to shape the gut's microbial makeup, and gut microbes make neuroactive compounds, including neurotransmitters and metabolites that also act on the brain. These interactions could occur in various ways: microbial compounds communicate via the vagus nerve, which connects the brain and the digestive tract, and microbially derived metabolites interact with the immune system, which maintains its own communication with the brain."

Ever have a "gut feeling"? That's a testament to this phenomenon.

So what causes poor gut health?

Processed foods and sugars destroy good bacteria and enable the proliferation of bad bacteria. Because western diets are dominated by this kind of food (if you can call it that), poor gut health is a widespread issue (and the cascading health problems that result from poor gut health).

On the other hand, natural, living foods provide a conducive environment for "good" bacteria. Fruits and vegetables contain prebiotics, which act as nourishment for healthy gut bacteria. And fermented foods contain probiotics, the actual healthy bacteria.

Don't underestimate the intimate connection between a healthy body and a healthy mind. And really, the body and mind are not separate at all, but one in the same. It's really hard to focus on the essential if your body is in a constant state of disharmony.

Lastly, we have the spiritual level. There is one word I want you to deeply understand and practice: MINDFULNESS. Mindfulness is being fully aware and immersed in the present moment. Again, think of anxiety as the gap between where your thoughts are and where your body is. If you're fully present, anxiety simply disappears. This is not easy for most people though, especially because people have been living in the future their whole lives and constantly distracted by tv, social media, to-do lists...etc. It takes practice to hone the muscle of mindfulness.

The very best way to cultivate mindfulness is through a daily meditation practice. If you're new to meditation, I highly recommend my mini-course **The 7 Day Meditation Challenge**.

When you can transcend the busy syndrome, get your body healthy and practice mindfulness, anxiety will have lost all power over you. Sure it may come up from time to time, but you will be able to let it pass, like clouds passing through the sky.

Mastermind Among Monkeyminds by Elliott Hulse

Note: This is a passage written by Elliott Hulse.

We live in a world filled with noise, distractions, and fillers.

Booms, buzzes, dings, pings, pops.

Constant text alerts causing your phone to vibrate, easily accessible music to eradicate any silence, and mindless advertisements cluttering the brain.

Where does it end?

What does this do?

How does it affect our precious brains?

A few years back when I was active on my YouTube channel (I'll be back soon), I received not a question, but an invitation from a young gentleman who had found "The Secret to Happiness".

Intrigued, I had to find out what this dude was spitting.

This young man had delved deep into searching for something that would make us happy, make us joyful, make us less anxious, jittery, and jumpy.

He had scoured through different philosophies, religions, and historical texts... and he found the answer.

Silence.

And before you start screaming swear words at your computer screen - try something.

Sit wherever you are with no noise.

Turn off your computer, turn off your phone, turn off your music and just sit in solitude.

Complete silence.

And see how long it takes before you grow uncomfortable and fidgety.

It's not easy.

We're so used to stimulus, people telling us what to do and how to think.

When we try to be by ourselves, ugly stuff comes up.

We may experience feelings of anxiety, agitation, anger.

When you're completely alone, you're forced to speak to yourself, to be true with yourself.

You'll experience years of bottled up emotion that you cast aside to the shadows.

Your mind may get cluttered with ugly thoughts.

But when you begin to experience those shadows of yourself and you deal with them properly, you're opening yourself up to receive endless peace, joy, and love.

And if you demonstrate the courage to deal with these shadows, you'll become a mastermind among monkeyminds.

Possessions vs Experiences

The following is an anonymous response on the website Quora to the question: "What does it feel like to be a self-made millionaire under the age of 25?"

"I've been featured on the homepage of Yahoo! as a millionaire, offered 3 separate reality TV shows – including that terrible Millionaire Dating one on Bravo. I bought a luxury car with cash on my 16th birthday, owned a house a few years later.

Hitting $1m was a non-event, I don't even know the exact date it happened. The dividends just all of a sudden added up, and it was there. I celebrated by buying myself a used Rolex. A few years later I also did a vacation where I "tried to spend as much money as possible" – but I still found myself gravitating towards "values" on the wine list rather than blowing it all out by spending thousands on a bottle, which I thought was silly.

Hitting 8-figures was a bit more substantial, I knew it meant I'd never, ever have to work again unless something went terribly wrong. The closing call with the law firm was one of the biggest anti-climaxes of my life. I had already "owned" the money in my head years before hand, so seeing it crystallize on my bank statement didn't make a huge difference, except that it freed me up to start tackling bucket-list items.

I had been postponing so many experiences with the idea of "doing it at some point in the future when I made it" that I just started tackling them one by one. Superbowl. Sundance. SobeFest. Africa. A month around Europe. 3-Star Michelin dining.

The only "awkward" thing I keep running into repeatedly, is other people's comments about wealth or money. Whether it's a tour guide pointing out a hotel that costs $1000/night and everybody in the tour bus gasps (and it's where I'm staying) or taxi drivers making snarky comments about millionaires, or people suggesting it's my "lucky day and I should buy a lotto ticket" – I run into it repeatedly and predictably, but I always tend to keep my mouth shut and not say anything.

Along the way, the most interesting phenomenon has been "adaptation". Moving from a $300K apartment to a $1m one barely made a difference after the first month.

Jumping from that to something 60% bigger, and oceanfront (on the beach) that was worth over $2m barely made a blip after the first few weeks.

Buying a fancy, fast sports car – yes, I did it, but again people tend to massively overestimate the "joy" or "happiness" that a particular item will give them vs. reality. After a few weeks, it just sits there. The anticipation, wait and planning is almost better than the realization of the event itself.

When they say "it's all about the journey, rather than the destination" that's absolutely true. The part that I've most enjoyed is hanging out, meeting and become friends with amazing, successful, smart and ambitious entrepreneurs. It's inspiring, invigorating, and just plain fun.

I still don't have a private plane or NetJets card, I fly economy-class around North America most of the time, I don't even have a maid to do my cleaning. I prefer to buy clothes when they go on sale, and I cringe at people who waste thousands on Gucci-this or Prada-that. I upgrade my MacBook every few years, not every model. I still use an original iPad. I've never bought a new car (except for my parents). The biggest TV in my apartment is 42".

Experiences, even when they cost thousands of dollars a day, so far have been my best investments. I've stopped postponing as much as I used to. The best time is "now", but to be honest, I could have done many of these things much earlier, and on a lower-budget, and probably still had a great time.

Try this as a test–

Make a list of all physical things you would buy if you had $10 million. Let your mind roam free. Don't limit yourself to the reasonable.

It's not that long, is it?

And if you worked a decade, or more to earn that money, you'd cross 90% off the items off that list anyway. There are amazingly few physical things that are worth spending money off once you've covered the basics. If I gave you $100K in cash and told you to spend it in a day, you'd be hard pressed unless you bought jewelry, or a car.

Gadgets? Clothes? A bigger TV? Unless money fell from the sky into your lap, you're probably going to be quite pragmatic about what you invest in. There's a reason why most lottery winners end up bankrupt within a few years.

The utility of money once you get past a certain threshold is very limited. And I honestly think that most people who want to be "rich" don't really mean it. What they are really saying is that they'd like someone to hand them a check.

But when push comes to shove, and there's hard work, sacrifices, and tears involved, they'd rather spend 4-hours a day watching TV along with the rest of America."

Inferiority Conditioning

A feeling of inferiority is a massive roadblock for most people. It is a roadblock for success, peace of mind, confidence, authenticity and the ability to just BE.

There are also billions of dollars made off of people feeling inferior. Look at beauty products, cars, clothes, jewelry and many other industries. A lot of them basically say, "Buy our product to feel good about yourself."

So why do so many people have this inferiority complex? Because it's been embedded into our culture. So-called perfection is thrown upon us from birth through television, media, movies, magazines...etc. We're conditioned to believe that certain looks, styles and behaviors are valued while others are rejected. Not to mention that all of the images we see are highly manipulated (the people on the magazine covers don't wake up like that).

This mass inferiority complex creates a society of disempowered consumers; people that will buy anything to chase that feeling of worthiness. But guess what? You've been worthy all along, without having to buy or do anything.

Here's the truth: You're worthy no matter what. You don't need to look or act a certain way to get society's stamp of worth. Actually, your worth cannot be determined by anyone or anything. We're all brilliant, unique and worthy, just in different ways. Accept yourself - while always being open to learning and growing - and don't let the conditioning tell you otherwise.

Accept your own unique awesomeness.

Hedonic Adaptation

"The hedonic treadmill, also known as hedonic adaptation, is the observed tendency of humans to quickly return to a relatively stable level of happiness despite major positive or negative events or life changes." (Wikipedia)

With most things in life, people find that happiness doesn't last. The high of buying a new car soon gives way to status quo. The excitement of a promotion at work quickly turns into the anxiety of handling more responsibilities. That is the phenomenon of hedonic adaptation.

An extreme example of this is a rich person whose day is ruined because they were served the wrong wine at a restaurant, different from the one they always drink. Yes, hedonic adaptation can get ugly.

We each have a "set point" of happiness that we always drift back to. This is why people are constantly chasing that next thing that will finally make them happy or fulfilled; a new home, a new car, a dream job, the perfect romantic partner...etc. But the catch is that no matter what we do, we always go back to that set point.

So this begs the question: How do you increase your set point of happiness? There are two ways...

1. **Breaking Routines** – Try new things. Eat different food. Go to a dance class. Try yoga. Take a trip to somewhere you haven't been. Breaking routines shakes up the process of hedonic adaptation and, if done regularly, increases your set point of happiness.

2. **Inner Work** – By inner work I mean anything that gives you the space to just be. This may be meditation, journaling, hiking, walking outside, yoga, gardening, playing music...etc. When you consistently immerse yourself in inner work, you make your happiness less dependent on external circumstances. The more you do this, the happier you become, regardless of what's going on in your life.

McMansions and Depression

We've all heard the stories about people who seemingly "have it all" (in the material sense) yet are not happy.

There are so many cases of rich people being miserable that we have to reevaluate our belief that being rich automatically makes people happy. I'm not saying you can't be happy if you're rich. Of course you can. And it's definitely not fun to be broke. But the problem is that we've associated happiness with the external world. And that's not how happiness works. Happiness is intrinsic. It's an inside job. If you don't cultivate happiness from within, then no amount of money, houses, cars, clothes, romantic partners or vacations is going to make you happy. Happiness comes from within.

In life, there are three general factors that greatly help in creating a happy, fulfilling life:
1. Creative expression
2. Being of service
3. Human connection

We need to be able to express ourselves creatively to feel happy. As humans, we're creative beings. Creative expression is crucial for our well-being. This is why people who work in careers that give them no room for creativity find it unfulfilling and soul-crushing.

The second factor is being of service. This is obvious. It feels good to help people! If you're not helping people at all, chances are you're not going to be happy (unless you're a complete sociopath). And the third is human connection. We need to be deeply connected with other people to be truly happy. Sure, alone time is great, but the purpose of solitude is to come back to your relationships with more to give. Our relationships are crucial to our happiness. What's all the success in the world if it can't be shared?

If you learn to cultivate happiness from within, express yourself creatively, live a life of service and value human connection, you will be happy no matter what. Sure, you'll experience ups and downs. That's a part of being human. But in general your life will be fulfilling and joyous.

Wisdom From Henry David Thoreau

"Our life is frittered away by detail... simplify, simplify."

"A man is rich in proportion to the number of things he can afford to let alone."

"I wanted to live deep and suck out all the marrow of life, to live so sturdily and Spartan-like as to put to rout all that was not life."

"I make myself rich by making my wants few."

"Most of the luxuries, and many of the so-called comforts of life, are not only not indispensable, but positive hindrances to the elevation of mankind."

"Simplify your life. Don't waste the years struggling for things that are unimportant. Don't burden yourself with possessions. Keep your needs and wants simple and enjoy what you have. Don't destroy your peace of mind by looking back, worrying about the past. Live in the present. Simplify!"

Declutter Your Mind By Decluttering Your Living Space

I had a profound realization after I cleaned my apartment in New York City one morning.

The realization was that cleaning helped me to regain focus. When my apartment was decluttered, my mind naturally became decluttered as well. I straightened out my physical environment, and my focus returned as I went about doing this.

Reducing the physical clutter around me took me from dazed and confused, to feeling clear and happy. It helped me overcome the obstacle of overwhelm and set a positive momentum for the rest of the day (the hardest part is to actually get yourself moving in the right direction).

A cluttered living space results in a cluttered mind. Your inner environment is a reflection of your outer environment; and vice versa. Everything is interconnected. Everything influences everything else.

If you feel like you lack focus and are overwhelmed, remove the clutter. It brings clarity. It's a form of simplification, or essentialism, which makes everything else easier.

You don't have to clean obsessively or spend hours doing it. All it takes is a few minutes.

If you can't focus at work, try organizing your desk. If you lack focus at home, organize or clean your home. Throw things out, get rid of the unnecessary. It will make you feel lighter and less weighed down mentally. Even a small act of productivity can create a cascading effect.

Remember, it's all about simplicity. You don't have to be a neat freak. You just need to be organized enough to curb the chaos and reduce all the mental noise.

Life is a puzzle. When you organize the pieces, you gain more clarity. If the puzzle pieces are scattered, you can't see the big picture. Think about how overwhelming a pile of scattered puzzle pieces looks. Sometimes it takes putting a just few pieces in place to start seeing the big picture more clearly. Have fun with your puzzle. See the big picture.

Complicate to Confuse

"The definition of genius is taking the complex and making it simple." – Albert Einstein

We've all experienced the frustration that comes with unnecessary complication.

This complication phenomenon can be found everywhere from health to economics, and everything in between. People complicate things in order to sell or maintain power over others.

An example of this is the economic term Quantitative Easing. Sounds really complicated, right? It's actually not. Quantitative Easing simply means introducing new money into a money supply through a central bank. The finance/economics industry is notorious for creating complexity in order to discourage the general population from becoming financially literate. Most people's eyes roll over when terms like Quantitative Easing come up, and they automatically assume it's too complicated to understand.

The same is true with health. Want to lose weight and be healthy? Eating real, natural food and walking every day will get you at least 80% there. But there's nothing sexy about eating broccoli and taking walks. Plus, it's hard to sell something so simple. This is why people complicate things.

This phenomenon of over-complication applies to almost every aspect of life. Which areas of life feel too complicated for you? What subjects do you think are too complex to learn about?

Look for ways to cut through all of the noise and simplify. A great way to do this is to take (seemingly) complicated topics and distill the main points until you can easily explain it to someone else.

Try it out. You'll get better with practice. There's no need to be overwhelmed in the land of unnecessary complication. Keep it simple.

Decision Fatigue

Decisions, decisions....

We only have a finite amount of decision-making energy each day.

Have you ever made questionable decisions at the end of a long work day? Or have you ever not given something the proper thought it required at the end of the day? This is the phenomenon known as *decision fatigue*. And we've all experienced it.

The quality of decision-making gets reduced after any long session of decision-making. And yes, our days are indeed long sessions of decision-making.

Then how do we avoid decision fatigue? Or at least minimize it? It all goes back to focusing on the essential. Think about how exhausting it would be if getting dressed, eating breakfast and every other part of a morning routine were big, complex decisions. For most people, this would leave them mentally exhausted before they even went to work. Yet we all do this to ourselves to different extents.

The more decisions you have to make, the harder it is to do the things you really want to do. Do you think Stephen King frets about how his outfit looks every day? Of course not, he focuses on writing. Because that's what is essential to him.

Automate the areas of life that aren't important to you. Leave the decision-making for the essential aspects of your life. This will allow you to avoid the energy drainage that most people fall into. In doing so, you will be able to devote more resources to the things you deem as essential. And that shift is what separates the amateurs from the pros.

The 80/20 Principle

This is a principle that most people are familiar with, yet few actually apply.

The 80/20 principle, also known as the Pareto Principle, is named after the Italian economist Vilfredo Pareto. Pareto came up with this principle when he observed that approximately 80% of the land in Italy was owned by 20% of the population; as well as observing that 20% of the peapods in his garden contained 80% of the peas.

This is why the 80/20 principle is also known as the law of the vital few. It's the phenomenon that the vast majority of effects are due to a small percentage of causes.

And this phenomenon applies to all aspects of life! Understanding and applying the 80/20 principle is like a life hack for success in anything.

Here are some business examples. Let's say 80% of profits come from 20% of products/services. In knowing this, you can focus more on that 20% and multiply your profits. Maybe 80% of complaints come from 20% of customers. You might want to market to a different demographic besides that 20%. Maybe 80% of growth comes from 20% of actions taken. Focus on that 20% and increase growth exponentially.

Here are some personal examples. Maybe 80% of your happiness (which is hard to measure, but you can still apply this principle) comes from 20% of your activities. Maybe 80% of your workout results come from 20% of your workouts. Maybe 80% of your wasted time comes from 20% of activities (*cough* tv and social media *cough*).

By understanding and applying the 80/20 principle, you'll be able to simplify, get more of what you want and less of what you don't.

Too Many Cups = None Get Filled

Here's a little metaphor...

Let's say that your goals, ideas, dreams and desires are represented by cups. Each goal, idea, dream or desire equals one cup. Now imagine your energy and resources as a pitcher filled with water. In order to bring a goal to fruition, you must fill the cup with the pitcher.

If you have too many goals, you simply won't be able to fill them all. Actually, they'll all just have a little bit of water. So nothing will truly get done.

But if you focus on one, you'll have more than enough resources to fill that cup.

Like all metaphors, this isn't perfect, yet it clearly demonstrates the concept. It's like the old saying, "If you chase multiple rabbits, you won't catch any."

The lesson here is the overarching lesson of this book: Focus on the Essential.

Wisdom Potpourri

"Simplicity involves unburdening your life, and living more lightly with fewer distractions that interfere with a high quality life, as defined uniquely by each individual." – Linda Breen Pierce

"Beware the barrenness of a busy life." - Socrates

"Slow down and remember this: Most things make no difference. Being busy is a form of laziness—lazy thinking and indiscriminate action." - Tim Ferriss

"Wealth consists not in having great possessions, but in having few wants." - Epictetus

"Perfection is achieved, not when there is nothing more to add, but when there is nothing left to take away." - Antoine de Saint-Exupery

"Reduce the complexity of life by eliminating the needless wants of life, and the labors of life reduce themselves." - Edwin Way Teale

"Besides the noble art of getting things done, there is the noble art of leaving things undone. The wisdom of life consists in the elimination of non-essentials." - Lin Yutang

"Smile, breathe and go slowly." - Thich Nhat Hanh

The Openhanded Life

Do you feel the need to clutch onto everything you desire?

Most of us do. We've been conditioned that we must grab what we want and hold onto it for dear life. This applies to everything, from our identity, to our goals, to our relationships, to money, and everything in between.

What if I told you that life is more about letting go than holding on? Well, that is if you want to be happy, fulfilled, present and at peace. If you want to cause yourself more suffering, feel free to stop reading now.

Enter: Openhandedness

Openhandedness is characterized by releasing that fearful, egoic clinging to everything, letting go, generously giving and cultivating the ability to receive.

An open hand can both give and receive, while a closed fist can do neither. If we look at the two basic motivating forces, fear and love, openhandedness is based in love while a closed fist is based in fear. Fear is constricting, an inhibitor to growth and a creator of unnecessary barriers. Love is opening. Love is growth. Love is freedom.

Openhandedness doesn't necessarily mean walking around with your hands out 24/7 like you're a Jesus figurine or something. It's a metaphor for your general mindset. If you're always so constricted and closed-off, you'll never have the opportunity to give or receive. A closed fist is also used to cling onto things. And so many of us desperately cling to every part of our lives, for fear of losing whatever it is we're clinging to. This is absolutely exhausting and completely driven by fear and scarcity.

"Let go or be dragged." – Zen Proverb

What happens when you cling to a person too much? They feel suffocated and push you away. What happens when you cling to your money? You drive yourself crazy worrying about it, poison your relationships and cut yourself off to making more. What happens when you cling to your identity? You end up pigeonholing yourself and block any spontaneity or change from coming into your life.

This is the mode that most people live in, especially in modern western society. I was completely controlled by this mentality myself until fairly recently. It's a byproduct of being possessed by the ego, living in fear and not trusting the process of life. That's a miserable way to go through life.

Yet a magical shift happens once you allow yourself to let go and trust the process of life. That which is meant to come comes and that which is meant to go goes. When you live an openhanded life, you give generously, receive often and joyfully flow with the unfoldment of each moment as it arises. Good things come and go, their beautiful fleetingness thoroughly enjoyed. Challenges are adeptly addressed then let go of. Situations come and go. People come and go. Those who remain in your life remain because they truly want to, not because you fearfully cling onto them. The openhanded life is beautiful, free flowing and rooted in unconditional love.

Lupe Fiasco has a brilliant reference to openhandedness in his song They. Resurrect. Over. New, saying "It's a new year, every time I open my hands." When you live an openhanded life, you're rebirthing yourself in every moment. You're effortlessly allowing life to spontaneously unfold and dynamically change.

Keep in mind that openhandedness is not synonymous with inaction. When you're openhanded, you align your actions with the flow of life. You harmonize all aspects of your being instead of letting your ego try to control every situation.

You see, openhandedness compliments essentialism. Without clutching onto everything, you're able to let go of the non-essential and transcend the trivialities keeping you distracted. By being open, you're able to fully meet every moment as it comes, with total focus.

Openhandedness is the open door through which you can step into the space of Essentialism.

The Key Question

Here's the key question to constantly ask yourself: *"Am I investing in the right activities?"*

At this point, you have a sense of purpose. And you know what serves you and your purpose, as well as what doesn't serve you and your purpose.

So with whatever you're doing, ask yourself, *"Am I investing in the right activities?"*

Check in with yourself throughout the day with this question.

Set reminders if you need to. Set a reminder on your phone, keep a post-it note on your desk, or whatever helps you to consider that question throughout the day.

If you catch yourself frittering away time on trivial things, don't beat yourself up. Just establish awareness, get clear on an essential activity you can do right now, and move to that essential activity.

Awareness is crucial. Once you're aware of how your investing your time, you have the power of choice.

Choose to focus on the essential.

Your Best Moments

Pause for a second. Now think about the best moments of your life...

Let them flash into your awareness. Visualize them...

Chances are, they were moments of Essentialism: watching sunset on the beach, being on top of a beautiful mountain, celebrating with friends and family, witnessing the birth of a child, having amazing sex with your partner, being in flow state while playing a sport or writing a book, traveling to a new place, meeting a new best friend, eating your favorite food...etc.

All of these things are Essentialism in action! All of the fears, stresses, anxieties, worries, judgment, burdens and trivial matters are stripped away and you're left with the pure essence of being in the moment.

In these moments, you know that there is nothing you would rather be doing. And that is incredibly rewarding.

And you don't have to wait for the weekend or your next vacation to do this. This state is accessible at all times. By practicing the philosophy of Essentialism, you allow the unnecessary to fall away and you're left with peace, bliss, fulfillment, love and the magic of being immersed in the present moment.

Life is Essential.

Did You Enjoy This Book? Leave a Review

If you found value from this book, please consider leaving a review. Reviews are immensely helpful and enhance a book's visibility. With more reviews, this book will reach and help more people.

Thank you.

Stephen Parato
Chief Fun Officer
FeelinGoodFeelinGreat.com

Made in the USA
Columbia, SC
31 October 2017